Anonymous

First Presbyterian Church Fort Wayne, Indiana Trustees Record

No. 1, Apr. 12, 1843 to Dec. 22, 1868

Anonymous

First Presbyterian Church Fort Wayne, Indiana Trustees Record
No. 1, Apr. 12, 1843 to Dec. 22, 1868

ISBN/EAN: 9783337381233

Printed in Europe, USA, Canada, Australia, Japan

Cover: Foto ©Lupo / pixelio.de

More available books at **www.hansebooks.com**

Before me the undersigned an acting notary public within and for the county of Allen, personally appeared Samuel Hanna, Charles E. Sturges, Allen Hamilton, John E. Hill and John Cochran, Trustees of the first Presbyterian Church at Fort Wayne who on their solemn oath say they faithfully discharge their duties as Trustees of said Presbyterian at Fort Wayne according to the best of their ability ____ ____

___ ___ before me the 12th day of April 1843

G. C. Lefferds
Notary Public

At a _____ held on the 12th day of April 1843 Samuel Hanna, Allen Hamilton John E. Hill, John Cochran, Charles E. Sturges Trustees of the first Presbyterian church at Fort Wayne appointed by the act of the general assembly of the State of Indiana approved January 25th 1843 met and were present as such trustees

On motion of Charles E. Sturges, Samuel Hanna was appointed President of this _____ of trustees John E. Hill Treasurer and Allen Hamilton Secretary

On motion of Allen Hamilton Samuel Hanna and John Cochran were appointed a committee to rent the farms devised by David Hughes to the 1st Presbyterian church ____

On motion of said Hamilton Charles E. Sturges and John E. Hill are appointed a committee to inquire into the terms of

On motion of Charles E Sturgis
~~the~~ the secretary is directed to
serve a request to the Selectmen Hamilton
~~to have~~ a collection taken up in
the churches once a month to defray
the expenses of the churches of lightly
~~feed~~ ~~after~~

On motion of John Cochran, It
Resolved that the middle tier of ~~free~~
pews in the church be rented for one
year, to the highest bidder, the
same to be classed as follows, to wit:
? middle seats to be rented at not less than
~~seven~~ dollars each, All of what is termed
the 2d choice seats are not less than five
dollars, and six of what is termed 3d rate
seats are not less than three dollars each,
the renting to take place at the church
next ~~to~~ tuesday week

It is moved that John E Hall
be appointed to procure a deed from
the county of Allen for the 1st of
ground on which the ~~it~~ church is
situated

James Bremer retiring from the chair

Pendent Motion

On motion of John Cochran, it is ordered that thirty feet off the west side of lot Number seven of Hanna's addition to the town of Fort Wayne at the sum of One Hundred twenty eight Dollars and give this note or statement of this corporation for the same —

It is moved by Geo. E. Sturgis, that John & Geo procure a survey for the above described lot No 7. and for a piece of ground in fractional lot, back of the same known no matter by Saml Hanna known as fractional lot 273

Samuel Hanna returned and resumed the chair

and the Board adjourned until Tuesday next unless sooner called

William Rockhill ?
Secty —

Saml. Hanna Prest

Tuesday 25th April 1843 The Trustees of the
first Presbyterian Church of Fort Wayne met in the
office of Samuel Hanna in the town of Fort Wayne
Pursuant to adjournment of yesterday. Present
Samuel Hanna John E Hill John Cochran
and Allen Hamilton

Whereupon the Trustees settled with the Revᵈ
J Franklin for the balance due him for his
services as Pastor of the first Presbyterian Church
up to 1st September 1842, and agreed upon
the balance as due to Mr Franklin at
two hundred dollars
                              Sam'l Hanna Prest
Allen Hamilton Secty

Monday 23ᵈ day of October 1843 the trustees
of the first Presbyterian Church of Fort Wayne
Met at the office of Samuel Hanna in the
town of Fort Wayne Present, Samuel Hanna
John E Hill John Cochran Allen Hamilton trustees
when Mr Franklin being present he acknowledged
to have received of Jesse L Williams the sum of
Sixty dollars, in May last also twenty five
dollars from Jesse L Williams in the
month of September last, also five dollars
from John Eagle, also two dollars fifty cents
from Saml Hanna, also five dollars from John
Cochran credit on Hamilton & Williams store, and
three dollars for Jesse L Williams credit in same store — making One
hundred dollars, to be deducted from the sum
due him up to 1842 leaving yet due him
one hundred dollars —

At a meeting of the church & Congregation of the First Presbyterian Church in Fort Wayne Allen Co Indiana Nov 25. 1845 agreable to a Notice given from the Pulpit by Mr Dickson. Saml Hanna was called to the chair & Joseph L Williams appointed Secy

On motion of Saml Bigger the following persons were unanimously Elected Trustees of said church to serve for one year & until their successors are duly elected. Saml Hanna. Charles E Sturgis. Jas H Robinson. Robt W Townley & Benj H Ferrer. On motion the meeting adjourned of Jas H Robinson It was

Resolved, That the Trustees be advised to obtain a subscription of $1000. the present year from the members of this Congregation to defray its expenses & for the settlement of claims against the same

Resolved, that the Trustees make an estimate to the best of their Judgment the proper proportion for each person to pay towards the expenses of this Congregation & endeavour to obtain subscriptions accordingly

Resolved that this congregation will meet annually on the first Monday in Jany for the Election of Trustees & the transaction of its annual business at which meeting the Trustees shall make a report of their receipts & expenditures & the situation of the finance of the Congregation

Resolved. That a collection be taken up the 1st Monday in each month to aid in defraying the expenses of the Congregation

Resolved. That in order to facilitate the duties of the Trustees we will call on their Treasurer & pay our respective subscriptions quarterly

On motion adjourned

Saml Hanna Chairman

J L Williams Secy

At a meeting of the Trustees of the first Presbyterian Church held at Judge Hanna's office on Thursday evening Dec 5. 1844 present Saml Hanna, Jas H Robinson. B H Town & Robt W Townley. On motion of Jas H Robinson Saml Hanna was elected President & Robt W Townley Secretary & Treasurer

Resolved that Saml Hanna & B H Town be a committee to employ a Sexton

Resolved that Jas H Robinson & Robt W Townley be a committee to make out an apportionment of what each member of the Congregation should pay according to a resolution of the Congregation at a previous meeting

adjourned

Robt W Townley Secy   Saml Hanna Prest

At a meeting of the Trustees held at S Hanna's office present S Hanna. J H Robinson, B H Town & R W Townley. Resolved that Mr Messhow be employed as Sexton for the present at $1 pr Week. The Sexton shall ring the church Bell at all meetings twice when there is preaching & once for all other meetings & whenever an alarm of fire is given. It shall be his duty to scrub the church once a quarter & always on Friday preceding the communion Sabbath. to sweep & dust the church every ~~Sabbath~~ Saturday. It shall be his duty to fill clean & light the lamps when necessary, & attend to the fire, & see that the house is comfortable. the wood to be furnished in the basement ready for burning he is to be allowed extra for Scrubbing the house

F. Wayne Dec 12. 1845

R W Townley Secy.   S Hanna, Prest

At a meeting of the Congregation of the first Presby
Church of Fort Wayne Aug 11. 1845

On motion of Dr Ayres. James Humphrey was
called to the chair & Ino Hough Jr appointed Secy

Judge Hanna then stated the object of the meeting
to wit. to learn if this Congregation would authorize
the Trustees of the church to purchase a new site
directly opposite the one already purchased for the pur
pose of erecting on it a new church building

After an animated discussion on the part of
Messrs Robinson, Cochran. Humphrey. Bowen. Bigger
Hanna & Ayres. It was on motion & adopting

Resolved. That this Congregation do hereby authorize
the Trustees of this church to dispose of the lot already
purchased & to by the two Ellsworth lots directly opposite
for the purpose of building upon them a new church
                                        adjourned
Ino Hough Jr. Secy   James Humphrey, chairman

At a meeting of the Trustees of the 1st Presbyterian church
held at Judge Hanna's office. present S Hanna. Jas. 16
Robinson, B H Town. C E Sturgis R W Townley — O N Sifford
a Notary public was called in who administered the oath
of office to the Trustees

Whereupon it was Resolved, That the Trustees of the church
will convey to Henry L Ellsworth the lot held by them
on the S.W. Corner of Berry & Clinton St in this city for
$600 & purchase of him 2 lots on the S.E. Corner of said
Street for $1150 & paying terms Cash $737.50. The lot first above
mentioned for $600 & the Trustees mortgage for $412.50 on the
lots purchased of said Ellsworth in payment for the same
provided said Ellsworth & his wife execute a good
warranty Deed for said Lots — adjourned
Fort Wayne Oct 20. 1845.
R W Townley Secy

State of Indiana } ss
Allen County }

Personally appeared before
me C. W. Seffords a Notary Public
in and for said County— Samuel Hanna,
James H. Robinson, Charles E. Sturgis,
Benjamin H. Tower and Robert W. Townley—
who being duly sworn upon their oath de-
-clar that they will faithfully and impar-
-tially discharge the duties of their office
as Trustees of the First Presbyterian
Church in the City of Fort Wayne according to the best of their abilities and judgment.

Given under my hand and Seal
Notarial this 21st October A.D. 1845—.

C. W. Seffords Notary Public

At a meeting of the Trustees of the 1st P. Church held
at the House of our pastor, present S Hanna. J. H.
Robinson B H Tower & R W Townley— it was—
Res'd that we as Trustees receive the donation of the
Presbyterian Board of Education. & that the thanks of
the church be tendered them for the same
Res'd that we agree to form a pastoral library & that this
donation be the foundation for the same
Res'd that this library be kept by the pastor for his own
use & the congregation under his charge
Res'd. That it is desirable that this library be increased
by donation or otherwise & that the Pastor keep a record
A J B.

Subscriptions paid up to this date   6,77
Various collections taken up   9,??
                                                               ————
                                                                0726,00

Paid 76 of Dickson   57¯59
paid Sexton   56.12
paid for Lamps   19.57
paid for Stove to Tyler   6.7¯
paid for Lights   25.21
Wood, Sawing & Coating Lucius   31.30
Cleaning Church   5.25   711.61
                                                        ————
                        In hands of Treasurer   8.41

We yet owe our pastor for the year ending
Oct¹ 1845   122.11
Balance due Mc Ellison as per bill from
Nov 24. 1844 to Jan¹ 1. 1846 including a charge
of $10 for extra services through the winter of 1845   28.78   152.89
                                                                ————
After deducting funds in Trea. hands we owe for year 1845 $142.48
        We yet have subscribed Considered good   56.00
                                Doubtfull   76.00

        Old debts standing against the Church
..te to David Archer   80.00
    5 Years Interest   25.00
B.all due Mc Masters as Sexton to Aps 1844   11.25
arrears of Salary to Mr Archison   103.56
Balance due on the Bell   15.00
Act to Judge Hanna for lot in rear of Church   150.00   354.81
        On motion of Judge Hanna a Committee of three were
appointed to nominate Trustees for the year 1846,
Committee Judge Hanna. Mr 76 Robinson & Jonas ?? ??? ?

Mr. Dickson proposed that the Creditors of the Church cancel their accounts. Whereupon the following Gentlemen gave the Amt attached to their names.

Mr. Dickson gave $50. Mr. Meekton $25. Judge Hanna, $53. Mr. Chamberlain his a/c $ B H Tower on Arches a/c $10.

J & McKinney on Bill $15. Mr. Anderson's bill paid by Hanna. Allen Hamilton & Sype & McKinney $103.

$84.51

Amt we owe after deducting what is considered good on note $6.45

411.29

deduct note 31st by Judge Hanna for lot   150.00

321.29

Amt cancelled as above   259.00

162.29

The Church is thus owing $162.29 Mr. Dickson proposed that a contribution be made, upon which

James W. Crumby gave	$30.	
James M. Robinson	10.	
Judge Hanna	10.	
John Cochran	5.	
Mr. Bigger	5.	60.00

Judge Hanna further agreed to see Mr. Archers & Mr. Hill, bills settled thus relieving the church from Embarrassment.

On motion of Mr. Robinson it was Resolved that the overplus accruing from the Communion Contributions be given to the Poor. — On motion of Mr. Robinson, the church consents to dispense with the usual monthly Collection — On motion of Mr. Bigger. It was res. that the Trustees be instructed to circulate two subscriptions. one for the Support of the Pastor, the other to defray the expenses of the Church — On motion of Mr. Robinson it was res. that the monthly Collection, for missions be given one third to foreign & two thirds for domestic missions & that we

Trustees of the First Presbyterian church of FortWayne, elected at the annual meeting of the congregation held at the church Jan'y 5 1846, Met & organized on the 13th of Jan'y 1846 at the Office of Samuel Hanna.

On Motion it was Resolved to have the following Officers for the ensuing year. A President, Secretary, Treasurer, three Collectors, to raise a pastors salary and One to raise money for contingent expenses

On Motion John Cochran was chosen President John Hough Jr Secretary. Jonas Tounley Treasurer

On Motion the following districts were set off in the exercion for raising the salary of Rev H. S. Dick on Pastor of the church 1st District. That portion of the city of FortWayne, lying East of Barr Street with B H. Tower as collector. 2nd District that portion lying between Barr & Calhoun Streets. S. C. Evans collector. 3d District that portion of the city lying West of Calhoun Street. J Hough Jr, collector.

On motion John Cochran was chosen collector for contingent expenses

On motion of B H. Tower, the place of business of subscribers. was chosen as the place on which to call on individuals for Subscriptions.

On Motion of Tower it was Resolved, to proceed immediately to raise a subscription for a Pastors Salary, and for contingent expenses and that for this purpose, each collector to be furnished with a separate subscription book and that subscriptions date back from the 1st of October 1845 and to end October 1st 1846.

On motion of Evans. the Office of Worthington Hough was chosen as the place of future meeting of the new Board. Members present at this meeting John Cochran S. C. Evans B H. Tower & J Hough Jr

Monday evening Dec. 28th 1846. Trustees met pursuant to previous notice. Present. Cochran Tower. Sounly Hough. Cochran presiding

On Motion, the note given Saml Hanna for $125. was received & cancelled, the Trustees having quit claimed to said Hanna the part of Lot no 7. Hanna's addition to Fort Wayne which lot was the consideration of said note. said note being dated April 12, 1843 signed John E Hill Pres & Allen Hamilton Sec'y.

On motion it was Resolved to take up an additional subscription for Pastors salary to commence October 1st 1846 & end Jany 1st 1847. the same being for one quarter.

On motion meeting adjourned to meet at the usual place on Wednesday evening Dec 30th at 8 O clock to prepare report for the annual meeting of the congregation

John Cochrane
Pres.

Ino Hough Jr
Sec'y

Wednesday Evening Dec 30th 18__
Met at the usual place pursuan
—ment. Cochran President. Prese
Tower. Townley & Hough.

Unfinished business was the
deficiency in subscriptions ascert
amount due the Pastor. determin
Motion meeting adjourned t
the same place on Saturday e
January 2nd 1847 to make fin al
the annual meeting of the cor
to be held Monday evening Jan__
in the usual place of worship
                              Hm __
                                P.

John Hough Jr Secy

Saturday evening Jany. 2
Trustees met pursuant to a
Cochran presiding. Present:
Hough Tower & Townley. Matter
to final settlement examined
report prepared. Meeting adjou
                              John
                                Pr
John Hough Jr
  Secretary

Monday evening January 4th 1847 pursuant to notice from the pulpit the Congregation of the 1st Presbyterian Church met for the purpose of hearing the annual report & the annual election of Officers for the ensuing year. On Motion James Humphrey was called to the Chair & J. Hough Jr chosen Secretary.

The evening being excessively stormy & the number present small, on motion it was Resolved that the annual election & other business be postponed one week & that this meeting adjourn to meet at the same place Monday evening Jany 11th. Whereupon the meeting adjourned

John Hough Jr.
Secy

James Humphrey
Chairman

Thursday evening January 11th 1847 the adjourned
meeting of the congregation was opened by prayer
by Rev. Mr Dickson & singing. James Humphrey
Chairman, John Hough Jr Secretary

The Report of the Treasurer of the Trustees for the
year December 31st 1846 was then read as follows

"Report of the Treasurer of the Board of Trustees
Jany 1st 1847 of the 1st Pres. Church. There has been
subscribed to the salary of Rev. Mr Dickson from
1st October 1845 to January 1st 1847 $915.—
of which there has been collected and paid
over to Rev. Mr Dickson the sum of $875.—
the same being amount of salary due from the
1st of October 1845 to January 1st 1847.
Leaving a balance uncollected & considered
good to be applied to other purposes of $40.7—
    There is due the Missionary fund borrowed
money to pay pastors salary   13.9—
leaving a balance in the Treasury in notes
for wood, orders on stores &c &c of $26.7—
There has been subscribed to the contingent fund
for meeting current expenses of the church $125.—
                    amount collected   114—
                    "   Received   114.2
                    There has been expended $105.—
        Leaving a balance to the fund of $ 9.0
There are debts, not presented, against the fund of
about $20. which could be met were delinquent
subscription paid.
    Foreign & Domestic Mission fund. Received
of former Treasurer April 25th 1846 $33.—
Received of Monthly concert collections up   ———
to January 1st 1846. inclusive.   32.—
                                                               $65.—

Amount paid Rev. W. S. Rogers agent of the

with a committee of three nominate trustees for
the ensuing year who reported the following persons
for the office of trustees for the year 1847 James
Humphrey John Hough Jr. S. C. Evans, H L Cook &
H. M. Cobison. an election being had they were
found to be duly elected
On Motion of Samuel Hanna it was Resolved
that the congregation proceed to the election of
two person to the office of Deacon.
After an animated discussion on the part of Rev
H. Dickson. Mefs Hanna, Robison. Williams
& Ayres as to the length of time for which
the deacons should be chosen to hold their office
the subject by general consent was left for future
consideration & reflection On motion it was
Resolved that the election be by ballot. A ballot
being had the following persons were found to
have received a majority of all the votes. I the
Cochran and John E. Hill were thereupon declared
to be duly elected to the Office of Deacon for the 1st
Pres Church of Ft Wayne. On Motion of Mr Robinson
it was Resolved. That the Session of the church
take such measures as they deem proper for the
ordination of the Deacons elected at this Meeting.
Report of building committee of the new church
edifice was then presented as follows.
The building committee submit the following
report. Total amount of the subscription list $7222.00
        Amount rec'd on subscription $5166.25
        "   " from Lutheran church 237.10
        " due on word now done   580.47
           Total amt expended $5983.82
Amount available on subscription $1207.69
" due from Lutherans on 1st pay't   162.90 . $1370.59

Painting	$225.00	Cash	$347.78
Stone trade	45 32	Stone lime	230 11
County Orders	50 00	Building Materials	327 69
Notes &c. &c.	82 15	Carpenters Work	29 80
Plasterers work	62 50	trade	107 69
Luthrans on P'pay't	162 90		$743.67
	$627.87 — — — — —		$627.87
			$1370.94

Out of the above we owe as follows

In cash	$130.00
„ Store goods	234.47
Stone lime & lumber	216.00
	$580.47
balance of available subscription	$790.47

Estimate of work to be done

Estimated costs of steps	$453.	353
„ „ Cupola	$650	
„ „ Basement	$1200	
„ „ finish cornish	$444.50	
„ „ making repository	$142.08	$2889.58.

which report being read was accepted on Motion.
After a long and animated discussion with regard
to the measures to be adopted for the completion of
the new church edifice & the proposal of several
measures, none of which were adopted, it was on
Motion of Samuel Hanna Resolved That the whole
subject of the completion of the edifice be referred
to the building committee and that they be
instructed to take the same under consideration
& to report some measure to an adjourned
meeting to be held at this place.

Where upon the meeting adjourned subject
to the call of the building committee

Monday evening January 18th 1847 New
board of Trustees met at the office of Mr Hough
and organized by the election of the following
Officers. James Humphrey President. John Hough
Jr Secretary. I. Hook Treasurer. Present James
Humphrey. J. Hough Jr. A. M. Orbison. S. C. Evans
& J. Hook.

The Treasurer of the old board then reported the
following funds in his hands. On Pastors salary
of last year. Town note $3.75 — balance due from
Barnett $10. do from Mr Griggs $10. from Mr Wetmore
$5.00 Order on Hanna $5.00. Chamberlains note
$7.00 total $40.75 due Missionary fund $13.98
balance of pastors salary subscription $26.76.
Cash on hand Missionary fund $18.93. due from
salary subscription $3.98 sum total missionary fund
$32.91. Cash on hand of contingent fund
amount subscribed uncollected

On Motion it was Resolved. That the English
Lutherans be allowed the use of the church for
public worship from three till five oclock on
Sabbath afternoons & at such other times as will
not interfere with the exercises of our own congre
-gations. On Motion it was Resolved that the
Secretary be directed to communicate the above
resolution to the officers of the English Lutheran
church. On Motion the following districts
were established in which to collect the pastors
salary. District No 1. That part of Fort Wayne
east of Barr Street. No 2. That part between
Barr & Clinton. No 3. between Clinton & Calhoun
No 4. West of Calhoun. Whereupon Hough was
chosen collector in the 1st District Orbison in the 2nd
Evans in the 3d & Humphrey in the 4th District
On Motion it was Resolved That the secretary be
instructed to move at the next conversational

that the collectors in the different districts be
directed to proceed at once take up subscriptions
for the Pastor's salary and that they report to
the board the results of their collection to a meeting
of the board to be held two weeks hence.
On Motion, the Treasurer was directed to procure
a suitable book in which to keep the accounts of
the church from year to year, and that he be
directed to post up in the same, the accounts from
the year 1846 to balance the same showing the
amount now in the Treasury
On Motion the Office of Mr Hough was selected
as the place of meeting of the board for the ensuing
year. On Motion the board adjourned to meet
Monday evening February 8th at the same place
at ½ past 6 OClock.

James Humphrey
President

John Hough Jr

Monday evening February 5th 1847.
The adjourned meeting of the congregation met
at the church Meeting being opened with
prayer S Humphrey Chairman & S Hough
Jr Secy
Report of the building committee
by S Hanna Chairman was then made
That the only feasible mode of raising funds
for the completion of the New church edifice
was by opening a new subscription for that
purpose.
On Motion of S Cochrane it was Resolved
That a new subscription be now opened
for the purpose of completing the basement
& cupola & enclosing the church.
After a long discussion on the part of
Rev H S Dickson, Messrs Hanna. Hamilton
& Cochrane it was agreed at the suggestion
of Rev H S Dickson that in case a sufficient
subscription could not be raised to complete
the basement & cupola & enclosing the church
that then a less subscription be taken for the
purpose of finishing the basement for a place of
public worship.
On motion of S L Williams it was Resolved
that the time in which the subscription be paid
& the manner of taking the same be referred
to the action of the building committee &
that they proceed at once to take up a subscription
On motion of S Hough Jr it was resolved
That for the purpose of meeting the contingent
expenses of the church a weekly collection
be taken up in the congregation each Sabbath
morning.
The meeting then adjourned "sine die"

Meeting of Trustees of 1st Pres Church of
Fort Wayne May 17. 1847

Present. Humphrey. Evans. Hough & Cook
The subject of allowing the use of the church
to Mr Little John for his temperance lectures
was then introduced on a written request
from the Rev Mr Mason before the
board. On motion of S. C. Evans it
was Resolved, That we approve of any
measures that will promote the cause
of temperance, and that we grant the
use of the church so far as we are
concerned in it, for the purpose named
excepting on Sunday. Wednesday
and Saturday evenings, provided the
consent of the Lutherans to whom the
church has been sold is obtained in
writing, releasing us from any responsibility
to them for any damages growing out
out of such meetings to the church

Adjourned "sine die"   James Humphrey
John Hough Jr   President
  - Secy

...... of eight dollars pr. week, be
allowed to the Rev James Greer for
his services as stated supply to the
church, during our destitution of a
Pastor

Whereupon Mess Humphry & Hough
were appointed a committee to wait
upon the Rev Mr Greer & advise him
of the action of the Board & request his
services & acceptance of the compensation offered
On Motion it was Resolved. that we
elect a Librarian whose duty it shall
be take charge of & regulate the
library of the church. And such
election being had Rufus Mc
Ferch was unanimously elected
and the Secretary was directed to
notify him of his appointment.

On Motion, Mess Humphry
& Evans were appointed a committee
to procure a suitable book case.

The Death of Mr I. S. Cook
Treasurer of the Board being brought
to the notice of the Board on Motion
of Mr Evans the following Preamble
& resolutions were unanimously
adopted." Whereas it has pleased our
Merciful Creator in his all wise
Providence to remove from this
...... Friend & Associate Isaac L Cook —

have also taketh away" that consolation
which we are incapable of giving. We
would recommend her to look to him.
who has promised to be a "husband to the
widow & father to the fatherless & he will
prove her comfort & her support.
3d Resolved That the Secretary be directed
to the widow of the deceased a copy
of these proceedings.
"On motion adjourned "Sine die"
                    James Humphrey
                        President
John Hough Jr Secy.
The above proceedings were handed
to the widow of the deceased accompanied
with the following letter.
                Fort Wayne. August 17. 1847
Mrs S. L Cook
        Dear Madam
                        As Secretary of
the board of trustees of the 1st Presbyterian
church of Fort Wayne I am directed to
hand you the enclosed copy of the.
proceedings of the board at their late
meeting. In complying with their order
allow me to mingle my individual
sympathies with theirs. As a friend one
who loved & esteemed your deceased husband
permit me also to hope that the source
of comfort hinted, may be indeed your

Meeting of the congregation of the [P]
[Presbyterian] church of Fort Wayne held
in the church Tuesday evening Nov 2nd [?]

        [Mr] James [Grier] being called up[on]
[& McIntosh] was chosen secretary.
After introductory remarks stating the object [of]
the meeting to be to consider the [question]
of selecting a pastor for the church the
[Moderator] opened the meeting with
prayer. After [the] introductory remarks
[of] [Judge Hanna, Robinson, & others, &]
[he] introduced the following resol[ution]
Resolved that a vote be now taken [to]
ascertain if this congregation is [now]
prepared to go into the election of a
pastor.

Previous to the taking of the vote, [some]
amendments were proposed by [Mr]
[Robinson & were lost]. On the reso[lution]
[as proposed by Mr Noel] the vote was
taken & it was decided not to go into
an election of Pastor.

On motion of [Mr Robinson] the
vote was taken on a Resolution to [invite]
the [Rev S Edwards of Montgomery & it]
& [was voted] not to extend him [an]
invitation at present

On motion of Allen Hamilton [it]
was Resolved that the ladies be
allowed to vote on the questions [before]
the meetings. After an animated
discussion. Hamilton, Hanna, [&]
[Lockhart & A] in favor Robins[on]
at some length opposing, the resolution
inviting the ladies to vote was carried
[...]

Hawes be invited to preach as candidate
before the church for the office of Pastor
for six months on trial.

The vote being taken it was carried
On Motion of Mr Hough it was
resolved that the same salary be given
Mr Hawes while preaching as a candidate
as was given to our late Pastor the Rev—
Mr dickson that is at the rate of seven
hundred dollars per year.

On motion adjourned "sine die"

John Hough Jr
  — Secy.

Pursuant to Public notice the annual
meeting of the church & congregation
of the 1st Pres Church of Portisague was
held in the church Monday evening Jany 10th
1845 for the purpose of hearing the annual report
& the election of Trustees. On Motion of J. Noel
A Hamilton was called to the chair & J Hough jr
chosen secretary Meeting opened with prayer
by J. H. Robison.

The annual financial report of the Treasurer
was then read On motion of Mr Tower, after
some remarks on the part of J. H. Robinson,
it was ordered that the report be accepted
& that it be spread on the records of the
Congregation

On motion of J. Hanna the chair then
appointed J. E. Hill. N. Chamberlain and
B H Tower a committee to nominate
suitable persons for Trustees for the ensuing
year, which committee nominated John
Hough jr. R. W. Townley. James Humphrey
R. M. French and C. P. Morgan.
On a vote being taken they were found
to be unanimously elected.

On Motion of J Hough jr. B H Tower
was appointed a committee to make
a collection for the payment of Mr
Stockbridge as Chorister.

"On Motion meeting adjourned
sine die"

A Hamilton
Chairman

John Hough jr
Secretary.

for the year ending December 31st 1857

Amount subscribed to Pastors Salary		$699.
Uncollected		15
Amount realized		$684
Collected from old subscription		34.50
Total realized for Pastors Salary		$718.50

There has been expended on Pastors
Salary as follows

To Rev H.S. Dickson		$350	
" " J.K. Canatta		15	
" " G.S. Hazard		16	
" " James Gier		144	
" " L.P. Hawes		145	$670
Balance unexpended			$48.50

Collections on contingent fund	$103.96		
Bal from old Treasurer	11.04	$115.00	
Total with Bal of Pastors fund		$163.50	

Paid out from the above

Refunded Poor fund	24.73	
Do Infirmary Do	14.00	
Do to Rev H.S. Dickson for lamps	22.00	
Acc of Townley & Evans	17.06	
" for Wood. Oil &c	28.87	
Sextons Salary sawing wood &c	56.12	$162.78
Balance on hand		.72
Uncollected balance	$13.00	$13.00
Balance available when collected		$13.72

There is due Mr Stockbridge
a. Chorister Sixty dollars for which no provision
has been made either by contribution or
subscription your Trustees recommend
that immediate provision be made to meet
this deficiency

The Deacons report as come into their hand
from the Treasurer for their Poor fund $24.5
and claims to the same .32.5

officers of the board for the ensuing year
Whereupon James Humphrey was chosen President
      J Hough Jr   Secretary
      R H Townley   Treasurer

On motion the following collecting districts were
established
— That part of Fort Wayne city west of Calhoun Street 1st District
Between Calhoun & Clinton Streets   2nd Do
   "   Clinton & Barr   Do   3d Do
East of Barr   Do.   4th Do
Whereupon
Jas Humphrey was chosen collector of 1st District
J. Hough Jr   Do   Do   2nd Do
R. M. French   Do   Do   3d Do
C. P. Morgan   Do   Do   4th Do.
    On motion adjourned "sine die"
February 3d 1848.   Jas Humphrey
                    Chairman

J. Hough Jr
  Secy

At a meeting of the Congregation of the 1st Presbyterian Church of
Fort Wayne held at the Church on Monday evening March 18th 18—

The same was called to preside, after prayer by
the Moderator. C P Morgan was appointed Secretary
who after introductory remarks by the Moderator stating the object
of the meeting — Judge Hanna — moved to take an informal
vote & ascertain the views & feelings of the meeting in regard
to the Continuance of Mr Howe as Pastor of the Church
which motion carried Ayes 68 Noes 22 — Thereupon Mr
Robinson suggested the propriety of taking the vote of the
Male persons present — when an animated discussion arose
between Messrs Cochrane, Hamilton, Tower, & Hanna — upon
the proposition of Mr Robinson —

On motion of Mr Howe, the meeting went into the election of
as Pastor — which resulted as follows, the male members alone voting
Ayes 18 Noes 11 and thereupon the meeting went into
an election — which resulted as follows 74 votes cast for Rev. Mr Howe
and 31 votes opposed, — (males & females voting) when Messrs Robinson & Judge Hanna made
some remarks — after which on motion of Judge Hanna it was
unanimously agreed that they press the call no farther.

On motion of Mr Robinson — after remarks by Messrs Tower, & Hanna
it was resolved that Mr Howe be invited to remain with us
to end a year from first appointment

On motion the meeting adjourned "sine die"

C P Morgan
Secy

At a meeting of the Congregation of the First Presbyterian Church of _____ Society held at the church on Monday _____ June 3 18__ late Communion for the purpose of _____ a Pastor to said Church.

The Rev. _____ Gill presiding as moderator. On _____ of C.S. Moran was appointed secretary pro tem.

On hearing of _____ bogus a vote was taken to ascertain the opinion of the meeting prior to _____ to the Election of a Pastor and decided in the affirmative.

It _____ to _____ proceeded to the election of a Pastor. Messrs _____ Brown _____ W.J. _____ acting as Tellers. When on counting the votes the _____ the Rev Mr _____ Wendldoffer received seventy one (71) and was declared duly elected.

On Motion of Mr Dr Cochrane it was _____ that Mr Wendldoffer be allowed a Salary of Seven Hundred Dollars ($700) per Annum for his services as Pastor for the ensuing year

On motion of J. Hoyt _____ Esqr it was _____ that the session call the Rev Mr Wendldoffer

No further business being before the meeting on motion they adjourned sine die

C.S. Moran
Secty

Annual meeting of the congregation of the 1st Presbyterian church of Fort Wayne held at the church on Tuesday evening, Jany 9th 1849.

On motion of Mr Cochrane I Noel Esq, was called to the chair.

On motion of Mr A Hamilton John Hough jr was chosen Secretary.

Meeting opened with prayer by Rev S. G. Lowrie d after.

The chairman then stated the objects of the meeting to be, the election of Trustees for the ensuing year and to hear the annual report of the Treasurer

The Treasurer, R. W. Townley Esq, then read the annual report, which after some discussion was adopted an ordered to be spread on the minutes of the congregation

The congregation then went into an election of Trustees for the ensuing year. and on motion of Mr Cochrane the chair appointed Mess Hamilton. Ayres & Chamberlain a committee to nominate proper persons for that office, who reported the following persons. John Hough jr. Oliver P Morgan Rufus W. French. Samuel S Dickason and Horace Davis.

On motion of Mr Humphrey the persons nominated were declared duly elected.

A deficit being found in the Treasury, after lengthy discussion between Mess Hamilton. French, Town

instructed to raise $600 by the usual
subscription; $900 for the purpose of the
support of public worship, and to pay
up the arrearages of the past year.

On motion of Mr Humphrey
Rev. Mr Kibeldaffer was requested to
urge upon the congregation from the
pulpit on Sunday the necessity of a
more general larger contribution on
sunday mornings to the contingent fund

On motion adjourned "Sine die"

Sim. Hough Jr   S. Noel.
    Secretary   Chairman

Report of the Treasurer of the Board of Trustees of the
1st Presbyterian Church of Fort Wayne, in the year 1845
There has been subscribed for the support
of public worship for the year 1845   650
already not collected   1045.—
leaving the amount realized   ....
            Amts paid out —
To the Rev. S. T. Howe for services as pastor
in this Church from Jan to Apl 10   "211.93"
To the Rev. J. G. Kibeldaffer for his expenses
when on a visit to this Church as a Candidate 30.00
To the Rev. J. G. Kibeldaffer on his salary
as pastor from July 1 to Jany 1   273.51
paid Stockbridge on part as Chorister   70.—   575.50
There will probably be realized about $50
from the old subscription, allowing this to be collected it
will leave the Church indebted to Mr Stockbridge   130.00
for which no provision has been made

_____ of _____ fund b.ll.cc.   145.39

To amt paid F. Bonneyman   13.53
  "   for Stoves Lamps &c   37.32
  "   F. W. Townley & as per bill 57.43
  "   Incidentals   6.75   147.53
     leaving a balance due the Treasurers,   1.64
We yet owe Sired for his services for the year 18.8 - 19.72
for which no provision has been made
     All which is respectfully submitted
                                        F. W. Townley Treas.

The Trustees of the 1st Presbyterian Church met at H. Durrie
store pursuant to a Call   On motion of Mr Horan
John Hough Sr Esqr was appointed President;
     On motion of Mr French - C. R. Morgan was appointed
Secretary of the Board   On Motion of Mr Durrie
H. Durrie was appointed Treasurer
     On motion the Collection districts as established last
year were continued & the following persons appointed
Collectors in the respective wards to wit.
Samuel Dickenson Collector for District No 1
J. H. Coughlin,   "   "   "   " 2
M. S. French   "   "   "   " 3
C. S. Morgan   "   "   "   " 4
          On Motion Messrs Durrie & Morgan were appointed
a Committee to employ a Sexton for the ensuing year
& report at the next meeting
          Ordered that the subscription be headed as last
year "For the support of Public worship" & that new subscription
books be opened
          Ordered that the Trustees see all persons, at their
next meeting, with the amount each would probably be

The Board met at the Office of [...] the meeting was called to order by the President when the minutes of the preceding meeting were read

The Committee appointed to employ a Sexton reported that [...] Brinsyman agreed to serve in that capacity [for] seventy five pr. annum   On motion [...] Brinsyman was appointed the Sexton for the present year—

The meeting then proceeded to apply such persons as they [...] would be willing to pay for the support of Public worship in the 1 Presbyterian Church—

This done — no further business being before the meeting they adjourned   sine die —

[signature]

of the 7th day of January 1850 —
On Motion of Saml Hanna, Smallwood Noel Esqr
was appointed Chairman and Rich Chute Sec'try —
After prayer by the Revd S G Rhiledaffer and some
explanatory remarks from Saml Hanna the
Treasurer H Duni Esqr submitted the following
Financial Report

Amount rec'd from Subscription $ 817 68
    "   by Weekly Collection   178 83
                                         $996. 51

Amount p'd Rev'd S G Rhiledaffer $ 720 74
   "   "   Mr Stockbridge   115 60
   "   "   Fred Benchin   94 72
   "   "   " Contingent &c   65 45 — $ 996. 51

There is yet due to
Rev S G Rhiledaffer   51 19
   " Mr L W Stockbridge   14 49
                         $ 65 59

And rec'd by Subscription for the board
of Mission from Nov 1/48 to May 1/49 $ 55 25
          "   May 1/49 " Nov 1/49   27 27
                                           $ 82 52

Which on Motion was accepted
Messrs Humphry, Hanna & Cochran were appointed
a Committee to present to the Meeting the names
of suitable persons to serve as Trustees of the Church
during the Ensuing year who handed in the
following names to wit, John Brown H Duni
H Morse H P Ayers & Richard McMullen Esqr the
Report was received and on Motion of Judy Hanna
Messrs John Brown Horace Duni H Morse
H P Ayers & Richard McMullen were Elected.

for officers yet to serve during the ensuing year
John Houghter was authorized and instructed
to make the subscription list for the purpose of
paying off church debt of some $3 per more
collected and more payment thereon

Robt W Tawnly Esq. made a verbal report from
the Building Committee, when after remarks from
Messrs Humphy, Cohen, Tawer Chamberlin Irwin
Brown & the Pastor it was on motion of S Hand
Resolved

That the Church be finished during
the present year (1856)
On Motion of Prch Chute it was
Resolved

That the building Committee be instructed
to finish the Church in such a style and
raise the funds to do it in such manner as they
May deem most proper
On Motion of John Hough Jr
Resolved

That Each Male Member of the Church
Consider himself as a member of the Subscription
Committee
Whereupon the Meeting adjourned Sine die
S Noel
Chairman

Prch Chute
Secty

February 11 1851 on motion of ___ ___ ___
was Elected Chairman On Motion John Brown
___ Richard McMullen was appointed Secty for
the Ensuing Year On Motion of SS Morss
H Devine was appointed Treasurer for the Ensuing
Year
On Motion of H Devine SS Morss was appointed
a Committee of one to wait on H Pays and
Know if he would serve as a Trustee or not
then being no more ___ the Meeting adjourned
untill next Thursday
Jan 11/50   Witness — &c,

W E H. McMullen
         Sec

At a meeting of the Congregation of the 1st
Presbyterian Church of Fort Wayne held in the
Lecture room of the Church on Monday evening
Jany 4th 1858. Allen Hamilton was called to
the Chair. John Hough k chosen Secretary
After remarks from Rev S. Edwards relative
to the seberation of the church & congregation
the Treasurer report was read, and on Motion
J. H. Chamberlain was accepted.
Mr Morgan then read a report from
the building committee, which after
some redbacks. was laid over for
further consideration.
On Motion, the Chair appointed
J. L. Williams. O P Morgan & Sad Story a
committee to nominate Trustees for
the ensuing year who reported the
following names. R. W Gourly. James
Humphrey. Rufus McFrench B. H Tower
& Charles Tressitt who thereupon were
duly elected.
On Motion of Jane Humphrey it was
resolved to assess the pews which have
been sold at Eight per cent on their
appraised value, and the unsold pews
which should be rented at 10 per cent
on their appraised value.
On Motion of Mr Bowen the question of
renting one half the free pews was
raised by a vote of 16 to 15 it was resolved
not to rent any of the free pews
On Motion of R. W Gourly it was resolved
that the congregation be requested
to meet the amounts due for church
expenses in advance for each quarter

At a meeting of the Trustees of the 1st Pres
Church of Fort Wayne held at the Store of
J W Townley 16 Jany 1. 1853.

Present James Humphry, Rufus M French
Beng. 1st Trene. Christian Tresselt & Robt W Townley

On motion James Humphry was Elected Pres
Robt W Townley, Treasurer & Christian Tresselt Secy

On motion the several Collectors were appointed
to the several destricts for the Ensuing year

On motion of R W Townley the meeting adjourn
ed Sine die

At a Meeting of the Trustees of the 1st Pres
Church held at the Store of J W Townley 16
Dec 12. 1853.

Present James Humphry. Christian
Tresselt & Robt W Townley. The object of the
meeting, being to take into consideration the pro
priety of appropriating the basement of said
church for the purpose of a Female School

The Pastor the Revd I Edwards stated
at some length the propriety of using the room
for this Purpose, as without it it would amt
almost to a prohibition in establishing a
Female School in connection with our church
as no other room can be had.

On motion of R W Townley the use of said
room was granted for the Present for the use
of said School. Subject to the control of the Trustees
of said church

Ordered. That the repairs necessary for the School
and all other expenses be defrayed by the School

[annual meeting of the congregation of the]
Presbyterian Church was held in the basement
of the Church Monday evening Jany 2nd 1854
On motion J Noel was called to the chair
and John Hough Jr chosen Secretary
Annual report of the Treasurer was then
read and accepted. On motion A S Mershon
S Humphrey & H P Ayres were appointed a
committee to nominate trustees for the year
1854 who reported R H Townly, John Hough Jr,
R. M. French. Wm Jacobs & Christian Tussell
who were duly elected such trustees.
On motion of R H Townly it was resolved to
increase the assessment on the pews to an
average assessment on the appraised value,
of ten per cent, on each of the pews.
On motion of Allen Hamilton it was Resolved
to increase the salary of Rev J Edwards as
Pastor from $800 to $1000 annually
On motion the Trustees were authorised to
rent such of the unsold pews as were not
rented, for such price as might seem in
their judgement most expedient.
On motion it was resolved to go into the
election of three Deacons two additional
& one to supply the place of John Cochrane
who in consequence of being an Elder
is as excused from duty.
After Prayer by the Pastor & remarks as to
the character of the men to be elected to
the office, Nominations were made and
ballot being had, Robert H Townly, Lewis
S Kirk and John Brown were declared
to be duly elected as such Deacons
No further business being before the
meeting on motion it adjourned sine die
                                    J Noel

Annual meeting of the Congregation of the 1st Presbyterian Church was held in the basement of the Church on Monday evening Jany 1st 185_ Deacon Wm S. Edwards was called to the Chair & C. P. Morgan was chosen Secretary — The Annual report of the Intermedialy the Treasurer was then read & accepted. On Motion of A. Hamilton the matter of indebtedness of the Church to J. Wool & the Rev. of Col M. G. _____, in balance by a fund or Church, was referred to the Trustees for consideration. On Motion of R. H. Townley Mess. A. Hamilton ____ & ____ Designee were appointed a Committee to nominate Trustees for the ensuing year (for 1855) who reported Mess. R. H. Townley, ____, R. M. French, B. Currie & C. P. Morgan.

On motion of ____ Morgan the Trustees were instructed to have the Church insured against loss by fire —

On Motion of Morgan Mr. Tho. Lawrence was appointed an honorary member of the Bd of Foreign Missions per life

On Motion of H. Chamberlain the Trustees are requested to collect the annuity on the Pews quarterly in advance

There being no further business before the meeting by adjournment

Finchie   Jonathan Edward

C. P. Morgan Secy   Chairman

Congregation met in accordance with previous announcement from the Pulpit, and was
opened with prayer by the Pastor Rev. J. Edwards.
/ Mr. A. Hamilton was appointed Chairman
and Geo. A. Sivic Secretary.
Rev. J. Edwards stated the object of the
Meeting and requested the Congregation to unite
with him in petitioning Presbytery to dissolve
the Pastoral relation existing between himself
and this Church, stating at length the Motives
inducing him to make the request.
On Motion (Esqr. Noel,)
Congregation agreed
to Comply with the request of the Pastor Rev. J. E,
On Motion
A Committee consisting of
Messrs Williams – Morgan – & Ayres – was appointed
to draft resolutions expressive of the feelings of
the Congregation toward their Pastor Mr Edwards,
On Motion (Esqr. Noel)
A Committee Consisting of
Messrs. Williams – Ayres & Cockram was appointed to
correspond with Ministers of the Gospel and others
in relation to the Supply of the Pulpit of this Church
On Motion.
A Committee Consisting of Messrs
Jacobs & Noel was appointed to attend Presby-
tery in this place, and make known to that body
the Action of this Church in regard to their dissolution of the Pastoral relation existing between Rev.
Mr. Edwards and this Church,
Committee appointed to draft resolutions
as to the feelings of the Members of this Church
towards Mr Edwards, Reported as follows:

The Congregation of the First Presbyterian Church of Fort Wayne, having been called together by their Pastor, Rev. J. Edwards, to consider the subject of a resolution of the Pastoral relation with a view to his acceptance of the Presidency of Hanover College, it is

Resolved, That we contemplate the proposed dissolution with sadness and view our bereaved consolation in the consideration, that in the Providence of God this removal of our Pastor will be to a position of higher and more extended usefulness to the Church at large.

Resolved, That in leaving the question of removal to his own sense of duty, and to the judgment of Presbytery, without formal and pertinacious remonstrance on our part, we cannot but refer with thankfulness to the Cordial and kindly relations which have existed between Pastor and people during the four years of his labors here, nor should we withhold an expression of our high estimate of his usefulness amongst us, a faithful Pastor, a sound and able Minister of the Gospel justly evinced in the strengthening of our beloved Church, and in the additions to its Membership.

Resolved, That his zealous efforts in the cause of education, resulting in the establishment amongst us of the Fort Wayne Academy, male and Female, so promising of good to our children and to the community entitle him to our warmest thanks.

Resolved, That in assuming the Presidency of Hanover College, should such be the result, he carries with him our kindest regards and good wishes and our fervent prayers that a Holy Providence may guide and direct him in all his efforts. God's glory.

On motion, Resolutions were adopted.
On Motion, It was ordered that the resolutions be published in

Pursuant to Public notice from the Pulpit the Congregation of the 1st Presbyterian Church of McWayne met in the basement of the church Monday evening Sept 3d 1855

On motion John Smallwood West was called to the Chair and John Hough Jr chosen Secretary.

On Motion of Samuel Hanna it was.

Resolved

That it is expedient at the present time to go into the election of a Pastor.

A vote being had the above resolution was adopted.

A ballot was then had for a Pastor and Rev John M Lowrie was found to have received Twenty five votes. Rev Mr Dickson one vote, and blank two votes.

On motion it was resolved to extend a call to Rev Mr Lowrie & that his Salary be fixed at One thousand dollars per annum.

On motion. J L William, J Cochrane, a H P Ayres, were appointed a committee to make the call in behalf of the congregation.

John Hough Jr
    Secretary

The annual meeting of the congregation of the 1st Presbyterian Church was held in the Basement of the Church, Monday evening the 7th of January 1852

~~_____~~ Notion S. Noel was called to the chair & John Hough Jr chosen Secretary.

On motion, without ballot, the old Board of Trustees were reelected without ballot.

On motion of James Humphrey it was Resolved That the Trustees be instructed to have the Church lighted with Gas

On motion of S. Hough Jr it was Resolved That the assessment on the Pews be ten per cent as the previous year

On Motion of R. H. Townly; it was resolved That $600 be raised for the purpose of Completing the Church by a committee consisting of Cochrane Humphrey & Henry Chamberlain

S. L. William then gave a verbal report as to the prospect of obtaining a Pastor

On Motion of H. Chamberlain it was Resolved That the Trustees be authorized to secure a chorister for the Children as soon as practicable

On motion of S. L. Williams it was Resolved That the Trustees be instructed to continue the insurance on the Church.

Meeting adjourned

John Hough Jr
Secy

~ Noel
Chairman

Pursuant to adjournment the Congregation of the P' Presbyterian Church met in the lecture room of said church and on Motion, J. J. Williams was called to the Chair and A.C. Prolasco was appointed Secretary.

The Treasurer presented his annual report which on motion was accepted.

The meeting then went into an election of Trustees for the year 1857 and the Chair appointed Sam'l Hanna John Cochran & H.P. Ayres a committee to nominate, who after consultation presented the following names R. M. French H.P. Ayres, S. McLaughlin J. Hough Jr & O.P. Morgan.

On Motion of S. Hanna, report of committee was adopted and the persons named, were duly elected Trustees for the ensuing year

On Motion of R. W. Townley, the Trustees were instructed to take into consideration the propriety of having additional lights in the church.

On Motion of H.P. Ayres it was as Resolved. That the congregation repay one hundred dollars of the money received of the Ladies of the congregation and used for the purpose of cleaning the church.

On Motion adjourned.

A.C. Prolasco   J. J. Williams
     Sec'y.   Chn

Fort Wayne Jany 3. 1855

Annual Meeting congregation was called to order by the appointment of John Cochrane Chairman & John Hough Jr Secretary

Treasurers Report read and on motion was approved and and adopted

On motion of S. Hanna the old Board of Trustees R M Trundle H L Ayres. A. McLaughlin. J Hough Jr and C F Morgan were duly elected trustees for the year 1855 by unanimous vote without ballot.

On motion of R. M Trundle it was Resolved That the Trustees be instructed to pro rata the indebtedness of the church on the Pews according to their value with a view to collecting from each Pewholder so as to liquidate the entire debt of the church

On motion adjourned

John Hough Jr   John Cochrane

Secy   Chairman

Fort Wayne Jany 7th 1859
Annual meeting of congregation
was held in the church On motion
J. Hanna was called to the chair
John Hough chosen Secretary
Treasurers report approved
On motion O Gorham. H. P
Ayres & J Humphrey were appointed
committee to nominate Trustees
for the ensuing year who reported
C. P. Morgan. Calvin Anderson
H D Israndiff. John Hough.
& R W Townley who were duly
elected. On Motion meeting
adjourned.
John Hough
Secy.

Fort Wayne Jany 4th 186c

_nnual meeting of the congregation
was held in the church On motion
J. L. Williams was called to the Chair
& C. P. Morgan made Secretary.

~~Treasurers report read and~~
approved. On motion of J. Hanna
the old board of Trustees were
duly elected for the ensuing
year. No further business being
proposed meeting adjourned

C. P. Morgan   J. Hanna. Pres
    Sec y

Annual meeting of the congregation
was held in the Church & on motion
S Axel was chosen chairman and
A.C. Prolasco secretary.

Treasurers report read ~~xxxx xxxx~~
and on motion approved & adopted
On motion OP Morgan, the Chair
appointed Saml Hanna S Cochrane
& Hd Bowen, committee to nominate
trustees for the ensuing year who
reported W Sharp, John Brown, M Mc
Alister & A.S. Brandiss and James Humphry which
nomination was approved, and
they were unanimously elected
such trustees, for the year 1861
On motion of S. Hanna discretion
was given to the trustees to assess
the amount of the indebtedness
on the Pews, to be collected by
assessment, from the Pewholders
during the present year.

A.C. Prolasco   S Axel. Chn
     Secy

Annual meeting of the congregation of the 1st Presbyterian was held in the church & organized by appointing I. Noel Esq. Chairman & A.S. Evans Secretary. Prayer by Rev. Mr. Armstrong. The annual report was then read & on motion was approved and adopted

On motion of I. Hough, the old Board of Trustees, Mr. Sharp, John Brown A. McAllIson, James Humphrey and A.L. Brandriff were unanimously reelected Trustees for the year 1862

On motion of John Brown. A.S. Evans & O. P. Morgan were appointed to assist him in seating strangers & others not having regular seats.

On motion the Trustees were authorized & instructed to remodel a portion of the seats in the gallery so that they could be rented

adjourned

A.S. Evans
— Secy

I. Noel
Chrmn

Williamport Jan'y 12. 186_

The annual meeting of the Congregation of the First Presbyterian church was held in the Basement of the church On Motion John Cochrane was chosen chairman & John Hough Secretary. Minutes of last meeting read and approved. Treasurers report was read & on motion approved an accepted.

On Motion of A. Brandriff, Jesse S Williams, A. Brandriff & H. P. Ayres were appointed a committee to nominate Trustees for the ensuing year who reported Joseph S Sullivan A. S. Evans, John Hough, Rufus M French, & H. A. Putnam who on motion were unanimously elected such Trustees for the year 1863 The Treasurer announced that a subscription had been raised that would liquidate the entire indebtedness of the church which announcement was received with much approval.

On Motion of Dr Ayres, the Salary of the Sexton was increased to $150 per annum, to commence the 1st of Jan'y. 1863.

On Motion. A. S. Evans, William Brown, & John E. Hill, were appointed a committee to seat strangers & those not having regular pews.

On Motion adjourned

John Hough   John Cochrane

Fort Wayne Jany 22. 1863

The newly elected Board of Trustees of the 1st Presbyterian Church for the year 1863 Henry N Putnam. Joseph L Putnam Amos S Evans Rufus M French and John Hough by agreement met at the office of John Hough and firstbeing duly sworn into office by Homer C Hartman a Notary Public proceded to organize by the election of Henry N Putnam as President of the Board Joseph L Putnam Treasurer and John Hough Secretary.

On motion John Hough was directed to prepare a deed for the old church lots 63 County addition & 273 Hannas addition to Fort Wayne in pursuance of the contract dated Aug 14 1846 & made with the English Lutheran Church

On motion adjourned to meet on call at the same place

John Hough
— Secy

H N Putnam
Pres

13   Fort Wayne March 10. 1863.
Board met pursuant to adjournment present. Putnam. Putnam Evans French and Hough. Deed to Lutheran Church reported approved & executed
On motion It was Resolved. That the salary of Rev J M Lowrie be increased to 1150 to commence Jany 1st 1863.
On motion Resolved That the salary be made by additional subscription. It —

Pursuant to Public Notice the Congregation of the 1st Presbyterian Church of Ft Wayne met in the Church on Monday evening Jan. 4th 1864. On motion J. L. Williams was called to the Chair and A. C. Probasco chosen Secretary

The report of the Treasurer was then read and approved & ordered to be placed on file

On motion of J. L. Williams it was Resolved That this Congregation agree to pay the Rev. S. M. McMue our Pastor Sixteen Hundred dollars as salary for the present year and that the annuity assessed on pews be increased to sixteen per cent on the Valuation

On motion of Mr Jacobs The salary of the Sexton was increased Twenty five dollars

The Congregation then proceeded to the election of Trustees for the ensuing year & On motion Mess Putnam. Whitman. Evans. Hamilton & Hough the old board were elected. On Motion of Dr Ayres it was Resolved That this meeting do recommend to the Board of Trustees if practicable to arrange the seats in the Basement in accordance with the best modern plan for the accommodation of Sabbath Schools Which resolution after some discussion by Mess Ayres. Williams. Evans was finally adopted

On motion adjourned.

Pursuant to call new Board met at the
office of John Hough January 26. 1864
Present Evans Putnam Nutman French
Hough who being duly qualified S.L.
Nutman was chosen President of the Board
and John Hough Secretary Bill of John
Astill for $35 presented or allowed
Claim of Sexton for Extra services
presented and rejected.
On Motion A.S. Evans was chosen
Collector of Church Contributions
H.N. Putnam was chosen Treasurer
of the Church with a Salary of $15.
per annum.
On Motion the Insurance was ordered
to be renewed. On motion adjourned
on call of President

John Hough   S.L. Nutman
Secy   Prest

Pursuant to Call Board met at the
office of John Hough Decr 19. 1864 present
Evans French Putnam & Hough. Nutman
absent A.S. Evans was chosen Prest Pro Tem
On motion it was Resolved to recommend
the following to the annual Congregational
meeting That Pastors Salary be made $2000.
    " Sextons do " " $225.
    " Insurance be made for $1200.50
On Motion The Secretary was ordered
to prepare a deed for Pews to be
given to such parties as required
them. On motion adjourned
John Hough

1st Presbyterian Church held Oct 13, 1864 in pursuance to public notice for the sale of Pews in the church as enlarged Saml Hanna was chosen Chairman John Hough Secy & O P Morgan stated the mode of sale. Each pew having a value fixed by a committee, the first choice to be ~~given to be~~ given to the party, who paid the highest premium, over that valuation. the second choice to the second highest bid, and so on. Premiums to be paid in stock, as far as held by purchasers & any excess over stock to be paid in cash.

H. N. Putnam Treasurer proceeded to offer the pews

			Pew	Premium
1st Choice	O. P. Morgan		95	$160
2 "	John Hough		65&66	330
3 "	Saml Hanna		97&98	" 360
4 "	Mrs E. Evans		61	180
5 "	P. Hoagland		93&94	266
6 "	S. L. Nutman		67	165
7 "	John E Hill		97&101	310
8 "	S. L. Williams		63&64	310
9 "	E. P. Williams		116	130
10 "	A. S. Brandriff		68&52	140
11 "	A Hamilton's Estate		68&69	
12 "	S. H. Robinson		92	
13 "	Saml Willis Hanna		90	$45
14 "	H. P. Ayres		71	25
15 "	Francis McElfatrick		124	
16 "	R. M. French		91	$10
17 "	James Humphrey		117	100
18 "	John Brown		119	100

No.		Name		
21	Thace	M. C. Shraff	121	$45
22	"	Kerdeuand & Going	122	$122
23	"	Sophia C. Noel	112	$30
24	"	C. E. Sturgis	113	$60
25	"	Wm Jacobs	44	$10
26	"	C. Bird	43	$10
27	"	A. C. Shobasco	13	$25
28	"	Horace Hanna	88	$40
29	"	J. H. Shraff	45	$10
30	"	Calvin Anderson	154	$10
31	"	A. S. Ferman	42	$10
32	"	C. W. Jefferds	11 & 12	30
33	"	Henry Hanna	40	1.00
34	"	Mrs S Chamberlain	145	.50
35	"	Alexander Wiley	16	5.00
36	"	Mrs. Rowal	10	1.00
38	"	J. C. Davis	38	Rent
39	"	A. Barnett Est	41	
40	"	A. P. Eagleton	96	160
41	"	J. L. Worden	143	
42	"	A. M. Orbison	72	
43	"	B. H. Forter	6	
44	"	A. S. Evans	18	
45	"	Wm Bowen	113	
46	"	H Chamberlain	146	
47	"	J. M. Lowrie	100	Pastor
48	"	James Story	125	
49	"	Mrs McMillen	128	
50	"	Mrs Ewing	89	
51	"	Mrs Forsyth	14	
52	"	Mrs Wines	15	
53	"	John McWilt	157	

congregation, held in the 1st Presbyterian Church, pursuant to public notice, on 2nd day of January, AD 1865. John Locke Lane, was called to the chair; & John Hough Chosen Secretary

On motion of Judge Hanna, the Old Board of Trustees, consisting of J. L. Nutman, A. S. Evans, H. A Witman, R. M French, & John Hough, were unanimously reelected Trustees, for the year 1865.

Treasurer's Report for the year 1864, & estimates for the year 1865, were read & adopted.

On Motion the recommendation of the Trustees, as to the following items, were unanimously adopted.
The Pastors salary, was increased to $2100.
" Sextons " " " " $225.0
Insurance " " " $1200.0

On Motion Samuel Hanna, assessment of Pews for 1865, was fixed at 16 per cent.

On Motion of Dr. H. P. Ayres an appropriation was made for the Benefit of the Sabbath School, of $150, and $200 if there be that sum in the Treasury after meeting other appropriations.

On motion, of A. S. Evans, it was Resolved. That a committee of three be appointed by the Chair to advise with the session as to reorganizing the Choir, by the selection of a new Chorister, and that this meeting make an appropriation of $250, for salary of such chorister for one year.

Ayres, Hanna, Cochrane & others meeting
adjourned sine die
John Hough
    Secy

Pursuant to call the new Board of
Trustees of the 1st Presbyterian Church
for the year 1865 met at the office of
John Hough April 1st 1865. present
J. L. Newman, A. Evans, R. M. French
N. A. Putnam who being sworn into
office by J. T. Watkins Notary Public
proceeded to organize by electing
J. L. Newman President & John Hough
Secretary and N. A. Putnam Treas.
On motion of Evans the salary of the
Treasurer was fixed at $150.
On motion it was. Resolved that
the Treasurer be instructed to
collect the excess over the amount
of stock bid on pews, in cash of such
parties as have not fully paid
for their pews.
On motion the Secretary was
instructed to prepare & have
printed deeds for Pews, to be
delivered when fully paid for
on demand, to such parties
as require them
        On motion. adjourned.
John Hough.
    Secretary.

held at the office of Johnston in g.
June 16. 1845. present. Whitman &
Evans. Putnam & Hough

Mes. Lowrie & J. J. Williams being prese[nt]
the former submitted the offer of
Mrs E Hamilton to donate $4.000 to
the Trustees to be used in buying for
the use of the church a lot fronting
80 feet on Calhoun Street & running
lengthwise on Holman street 196
feet to erect there a missionary
church & a room for a Sabbath school
the Trustees to give back to Mrs
Hamilton a declaration of Trust
as to the extent, uses & purposes for
which said lot was to be held.
On Motion of A. S. Evans it was
Resolved That the donation of
Mrs Hamilton be accepted for
the uses & purposes set forth in
the declaration of Trust.
On Motion of N. N. Putnam it was
Resolved that Mes. Lowrie & Williams,
be a committee to wait on Mrs
Hamilton & request a modification
of the terms of her donation.
The Secretary then reported the
form of deed for Pews, prepared
& printed for the use of the church
which was read, approved & adopted
On Motion of A. S. Evans. it was
Resolved. That all future conveyances
notes, declarations of trust and all
other papers necessary to the use of
the Trustees of the First Presbyterian
church for the holding and

... was executed & delivered by the President
Secretary of the Board in their behalf.
Meeting adjourned
John Hough
      Secretary.

Pursuant to Call the Board met
the office of John Hough Sept 23. 1865
Present Nutman. French. Putnam
and Hough. Object of the meeting
was stated, to be to consider the
propriety of increasing the salary of
the Treasurer. After some discussion
it was unanimously
Resolved That the salary of H. A.
Putnam be increased $50 making
his salary $200. Adjourned
John Hough
      Secretary.

Pursuant to Call the Session and
Trustees of the 1st Pres Church met at the
office of John Hough Oct 23. 1865. Present
J.L. Williams. H. P. Ayres. J. B. Nutman
H A. Putnam. A.S. Evans R M French
& John Hough. Object of the meeting
was stated to be to consider the
health of the Pastor. Rev S. M. Lourie
After much discussion it was
Resolved That we deem it the
duty of our Pastor to suspend for the
present his Ministerial labors
and that he take a journey for his health
& that for this purpose we appropriate
the sum of Two hundred dollars to

On motion I. S. Williams & J. S. Nelson
were appointed a committee
notify Nixon of the action of the
Session & Trustees. Adjourned
John Hough
　　　Secretary

At a meeting of the Congregation
of the 1st Pres Church pursuant
to due notice held on the 1st of Jan
1866. Samuel Hanna was called
to the Chair & John Hough chosen
Secretary. Report of Treasurer was
read & adopted unanimously
On Motion of S. S. Williams, the
old board of Trustees. I. D. Nelson
A. S. Evans. H. N. Putnam. R. M.
French & John Hough, were reelected by an unanimous vote
to serve for another year 1866
On Motion it was Resolved that the
Trustees be authorised to pay the
assistant Pastor Rev A. A. Morey
such salary as shall be agreed
upon with the Pastor Rev I. A. Lowrie
On Motion of A. S. Evans it was
Resolved That appropriation for
the Sabbath school of $200 be
continued for another year.
after some congratulatory remarks
from the Chair on the prosperous
condition of the church finances
the Congregation adjourned
John Hough
　　　Secretary.

...[Aug] 25th 1866 Board of Trustees of
[Pres]byterian Church met at the
[office] of John Hough pursuant to
[call] present Nutman, Evans, French,
[Nutm]an & Hough. Election of officers
[be]ing had S.L. Nutman was chosen
[Pres]ident & John Hough Secretary
[&] Nutman Treasurer
[On m]otion Salary of Treasurer was
[fixe]d at $200 of Sexton at $250.
[Where]upon Board adjourned
[sin]e die
[Joh]n Hough Secy

[Ju]ly 28. 1866   Board met at the
[off]ice of John Hough on the call
[of the] President. Present. Nutman
[E]vans. Hough & French.
[On m]otion of Evans the Salary of
[Re]v H Morey assistant Pastor, was
[f]ixed at one thousand dollars per
[ye]ar, & that the same be assessed
[on] the Pews, by an additional
[asse]ssment of four per cent on
[the] Pews in addition to the
[re]gular assessment already
[f]ixed.   Adjourned
John Hough
        Secy
[A]t a meeting of the Session and
[Tr]ustees held at the office of
[Jo]hn Hough held on the evening
[of] October 26th 1866 It was Resolved
[as] the unanimous opinion
[of] both bodies that in view of
[the] present state of health of

occasional supply and that all
for the present the Evening service
should be dispensed with till
such time as the Pastor shall
deem it safe to resume his full
labors. On Motion this decision
was ordered to be made to the
congregation

Wm Hough
Sec'y

Pursuant to Public notice, the
Congregation of the 1st Presbyterian Church
met in the Basement of the church
January 5th 1867. John Cochrane was
called to the chair & O P Morgan
chosen Secretary.
The report of the Treasurer was then
read and approved.
An election for Trustees for the
ensuing year was then had and
J. L. Nutman, A S Evans, H N Putnam,
K. M French & John Hough were
unanimously elected such Trustees
for the year 1867. On Motion of Evans
an appropriation of $100 was made for the
sabbath schools out of monies not otherwise
appropriated. adjourned.

O P Morgan Sec'y   John Cochrane Chrm

March 17. 1868. New Board of Trustees
met at the office of John Hough
and were duly qualified.
J. L. Nutman was elected President
John Hough Secretary & H N Putnam
Treasurer On Motion Salary of the
Treasurer was made $200 Sexton's $25.

cost of Sperm aces & on Bioleire were
instructed to purchase two of the
Chubbuck furnaces at a cost of $1
each each. adjourned
John Hough Secy.

Board met met Sept 9. 1867 absent
Evans. Hough & French were
appointed a committee to confer
with the different churches of the
city and to employ Counsel to
defend against the assessment
for sewerage & nicholson pavement
adjourned
      John Hough Secy.

Pursuant to Public Notice the
congregation of the 1st Presbyterian
church met in the basement Jany 13. 18
Dr N P Ayres was chosen Chairman
John Hough chosen Secy
Report of Treasurer read & approved
On Motion the assessment on the
pews for the year 1868 was fixed
at 2 per cent on the valuation
& that the Treasurer be instructed to
prepare a printed notice, to be given
to pewholders, stating briefly the
cause of the increase
The committee appointed to nominate
Trustees for the year 1868 reported
the following persons S L Nutman John
Hough. H. N. Putnam. O P. Morgan
& S. B. Root. who were unanimously
elected. On Motion the Trustee were
instructed to place iron columns in the

...on call of President
...Hough Secy.

...26. 1867 Board met at the office
...Hough full board present
Motion . I.T. Orbison was allowed a
...lary as chorister of $50. a quarter to
commence from April 1. 1867
On Motion of Evans a committee of two,
...ans & Putnam, were appointed to
consult with the Session as to employing
Mr Mead to drill the Choir, & to advise
with them as to the financial condition
of the church
On Motion the Treasurer was instructed
to pay Mr Evans Supt of the Sabbath school
$75 out of the appropriation made by
the congregation, at its annual Meeting
adjourned
John Hough Secy

Board met June 27. 1867 at the office
of John Hough full board present
On Motion of Evans the President was
instructed to sign a remonstrance
against building a sewer up Clinton
Street, past the church so as to be a
tax against the church.
On Motion. Evans was appointed
a committee to examine as to
the cost of stoves or furnaces for
the church to report at a future
Meeting. Adjourned
John Hough
Board Met Aug 31. 1867, absent Putnam,

...1st Presbyterian Church of Wichita, in the basement of the Church [?] 27. 1868 at 7 oclock to consider the question of the election of a Pastor.

[?] N. S. Smith Moderator, John Hough [Secret]ary, Opened with Singing reading the Scriptures & prayer

On Motion of Dr H P Ayres it was resolved to go into such an election

Tellers being appointed & a ballot had, Rev Thomas N Skinner Jr. LL of Staten Island New York had 58. Votes Rev J H Money 17 Votes. Rev Mr Reed. 6. Votes & Wilson 1. A Second ballot being had Rev Mr Skinner received 75 Votes. Rev Mr Money 5 Votes.

On Motion of S. L. Williams it was Resolved that a call be extended to Rev Dr Skinner to be signed by the Elders Deacons & Trustees, attested by the Moderator & Secretary.

On Motion of C P Morgan it was resolved that the amount to be inserted in the call should be fixed at Seventy five Hundred dollars

There being no further business on Motion of W H Jacobs the meeting adjourned, sine die, after the singing of the doxology & benediction

John Hough
        Secy

N. S. Smith
        Moderator

For further record of proceedings see page. 97.

... at a meeting held in the ...
... Presbyterian church in Fort Wayne March 10 1845
for the purpose of considering the subject of building
a New Church Edifice

On motion of Judge Hanna, the meeting
was organized by calling Mr. I. H. Robinson to
the chair. On Motion of S. S. Williams John
Hough Jr. was chosen Secretary
The Meeting was then opened with prayer by
Rev. H. S. Dickson

The object of the meeting was then stated, and
general remarks made as to the spirit with which
it should be carried out, by Messrs Dickson, Robinson
& Hamilton

On Motion of Judge Hanna, seconded by
Allen Hamilton, it was, after some discussion
on the part of Messrs Robinson Hanna Hamilton
& Mershon with various amendments

Resolved. That it is expedient that the
necessary preliminary measures be now taken
for building a new church edifice in the year
1846 for the use of the 1st Presbyterian church and
congregation.

After discussion on the part of Messrs Tower
Cochran Dickson Hamilton & Ayers, it was on
Motion of S. S. Williams

Resolved. That Messrs Saml Bigger, R. McJean
Saml Hanna, Allen Hamilton, John Cochran
& S. P. Stryker, be and hereby are constituted a committee
to ascertain the practicability of procuring a suitable
lot on which to erect a new Church and the
lowest terms on which such lot can be bought and
that they report the result of their enquiries to an
adjourned meeting to be held in this place on next
Monday evening

After discussion on the part of Messrs Hanna,
Robinson Dickson H. & W. S. ...

...tion of ... Williams ... resolved
... Saml Hanna, J E Hill, John Cochran,
... Tower, R M Townley, J H Robinson & J L William
... and hereby are constituted a committee of ways
... means whose duty it shall be to consider the
... mode of raising the necessary funds and to
... circulate subscription papers, and to report fully
... as to the whole subject of building a church, site
... plan &c and that they report at the adjourned
... meeting meeting.

 On Motion the meeting then adjourned
to meet again at the same place on Monday evening
March 24. 1845.
      J H Robinson
       Chairman

Jno Hough Jr Sec'y

 Adjourned meeting of the congregation
of the 1st Presbyterian church of Fort Wayne held at
the church March 24. 1845 for the purpose of considering
the subject of building a new church.

 On Motion Judge McNachen was called
to the chair & H. Irvine was appointed Secretary.

 Rev Mr Dickson then opened the meeting
with prayer.

 Samuel Bigger, as Chairman of the committee
to whom was referred the subject relative to procuring a
suitable lot on which to build a church and the terms
on which such lot could be had, then submitted the
following report and resolutions.

 The Committee to whom was referred the subject
of examining a site for a new church & the matters
connected therewith, submit that they find that the
lot on the corner of Clinton & Berry Streets commonly
known as the Mrs Jarrett Lot can be obtained at a
reasonable price, to Wit for the sum of six hundred
dollars on subscription, which the committee believe

... y ... prospect of ...
at least twenty feet in width adjoining to the foregoing
Lot whereupon your committee recommend the
adoption of the following resolution"

Resolved that the trustees of the 1st Presbyterian
church be instructed to examine the title thereto &
if satisfied therewith, to procure the title etc
aforesaid as soon as practicable for the use and
benefit of said church & that steps be also taken
to secure at least 20 feet in width adjoining the
west said lot.

On motion the above report and resolutions
were adopted.

Mr. Williams on behalf of the committee to whom
was referred the general subject of raising funds
& reporting as to the general subject of a new church
then reported the following Resolutions which
after some discussion were severally adopted

— 1 <u>Resolved</u>: That for the purpose of carrying into
effect the resolution adopted at the last meeting
a Building committee be now appointed to
whom discretion shall be committed, the whole
subject of raising subscriptions, procuring a
suitable plan, making contracts &c

2 <u>Resolved</u> That the following persons, form the
building committee provided for in the
preceding resolution to Wit. Samuel Hanna
John Cochran. R. W. Townley Samuel Bigger
John E Hill. Jesse L Williams & B H Tower.

3 <u>Resolved</u> That in arranging the details
of the plan, the following general outlines
be kept in view to Wit. that the building be
not less than fifty feet wide nor less than
Eighty feet long, with a Basement story for
Sabbath schools and Lecture rooms and
that the cost of the building be not less
than four thousand ... ($4000)

~~Resolved That the pews of the new pews~~
recovered from sale, and remain free for
the occupancy of any and all persons, Provided
that if at any future time the Trustees may
consider the number of free pews, unnecessarily
large, they may rent one half of them for
the benefit of the congregation leaving one
tenth forever free.

Resolved That when the building is
completed the Pews (leaving out the one fifth
of free pews) shall be equitably valued so that
their aggregate valuation shall equal the
whole cost of the church, including the
cost of ground and that they be then
sold to the highest bidder, taking the
valuation as the minimum price.

6. Resolved That in the purchase of pews
the amount which may have been
subscribed and paid by individuals shall
be taken in payment for said Pew or Pews

7 Resolved That each purchaser of a pew
after having paid therefor, shall receive
a deed therefor, to be held by him, his
heirs or assigns as other real estate, subject
to such uniform an equitable tax as the
trustees may deem it necessary from time
to time to assess to aid in discharging
the current expenses of the church and
congregation, said assessment to be based
on the original valuation, and such
taxes and assessments shall be a lien and
charge upon said Pews

8. Resolved. That the Trustees be authorized to sell
the present Church, lot & Building upon the best
terms, reserving profession of the same untill the new
church is finished, and the proceeds of said property

... Trustee Bigger it was

Resolved, That the Building committee shall so contract for the erection of the church or the church building that the contractor or contractors & all others shall not hold any lien thereon against the church in its corporate capacity or otherwise, for any work, labor, or materials done or furnished in and about said said building. And that in raising the means and paying for the construction and completion of said building the course pursued shall be substantially as follows. First A paper shall be circulated by the proper committee to receive subscriptions to be paid in money, labor, materials, or other property. Second the subscriptions so far as may be expedient & practicable, shall be so taken that the person subscribing shall be bound as soon as the building contract may be completed, to execute and deliver to the committee a note or promise in writing, for the payment or discharge of the amount of his subscription payable to the contractor or contractors for such church building according to the terms specified in the subscription paper, every such note or written promise, to be placed in the hands of the committee to be paid or delivered to the contractor or contractors, in the manner which may be specified in the building contract & shall be deemed in all cases when so delivered a payment to such contractors to the amount therein specified without recourse upon the church or its Trustees. Third if any subscriber at the time the Pews shall be offered for sale, shall have failed to pay or discharge the amount of his subscription or any part thereof, and the

...ews are offered for sale become a purchaser of any such pew or pews and the amount which any subscriber may be in arrear as aforesaid shall be received from such contractor in payment on such pew or pews.

After remarks from Mess dickson Hamilton, Bigger, Williams and Robinson the meeting adjourned "sine die"

H Dunn Sec

At a meeting of the congregation of the 1st Presbyterian church of Fort Wayne held at the church August 11th 1845. James Humphrey on Motion of Dr Ayers, was called to the chair and John Hough Jr chosen Secretary.

Samuel Hanna then stated the object of the meeting to be, to learn if this congregation would authorize the Trustees of the church to purchase a new site directly opposite the one already purchased for the purpose of erecting on it a new church building. After an animated discussion on the part of Mess Robinson, Cochran, Humphrey Bowen, Bigger, Hanna & Ayers it was on Motion of H. P. Ayers

Resolved That this congregation do hereby authorize the Trustees of this church to dispose of the Lot already purchased and to buy in place thereof the two Ellsworth Lots directly opposite for the purpose of building upon them the new church Edifice

Committee of the ..... church of Fort Wayne
held at the church on Monday evening of
the 26th 1852 Samuel Hanna was called to
the chair & John Hough jr was chosen
Secretary

On Motion of John Cochrane the following
Committee were appointed to assess the
value of the Pews in the new church
edifice in pursuance of the Resolution
passed at the meeting of the Congregation
held March 24th 1845.

    Committee John Cochrane. R. W Townley
& James Humphrey.

After some discussion it was moved
to have the dedication of the new
Church edifice on Sunday the 14th day
of November A D 1852.

John Hough jr   meeting adjourned
    Secy

At a meeting of the Session Trustees and
Building Committee of the 1st Presbyterian
Church of Fort Wayne at the Church Monday
evening Nov 8th Smallwood Noll was called
to the Chair & John Hough jr chosen Secretary

On Motion of R. W Townley it was
Resolved
        That in consideration of the
time expended and the great service rendered
by John Cochrane in the erection of the new
Church edifice the Trustees of the 1st Presbyterian
of Church of Fort Wayne be and hereby are
authorised and instructed to convey to
said Cochrane by deed in fee simple a pew
in said new building free of charge to
the said Cochrane said pew to be a choice
one according to the choice and selection

tion of Samuel Hanna Jesse Williams
John Saul, C P Morgan & John Hough
were appointed a committee to ascertain
the amount of the subscription list in the
erection of the building, the debts due for
the completion of the same with a view
to ascertain & report at a future meeting
the whole cost of said building.
                    Meeting then adjourned
John Hough jr
    Secy.

At a meeting of the Session, trustees and
Building Committee of the 1st Presbyterian church
of Fort Wayne held at the Church Wednesday
evening Nov 10th 1852. Saml Hanna was
called to the Chair & John Hough jr chosen
Secretary.
    J. L. Williams Chairman of the Committee
to ascertain the entire cost of the church building
with the cost of the lots appointed at the meeting
Nov 4th 1852 reported as follows.
"The committee to ascertain the probable
cost of the church building report that
they find it to be about $13500 including
the cost of the two lots on which the
building is erected".
John Cochrane chairman of the committee
appointed at the meeting of October 26th
1852 to ascertain and fix a valuation
on the pews in pursuance of Resolution
Number Five passed at the meeting
of March 24th 1845 reported
"In pursuance of the duty devolved
upon them your committee report that
they have made their valuation on the

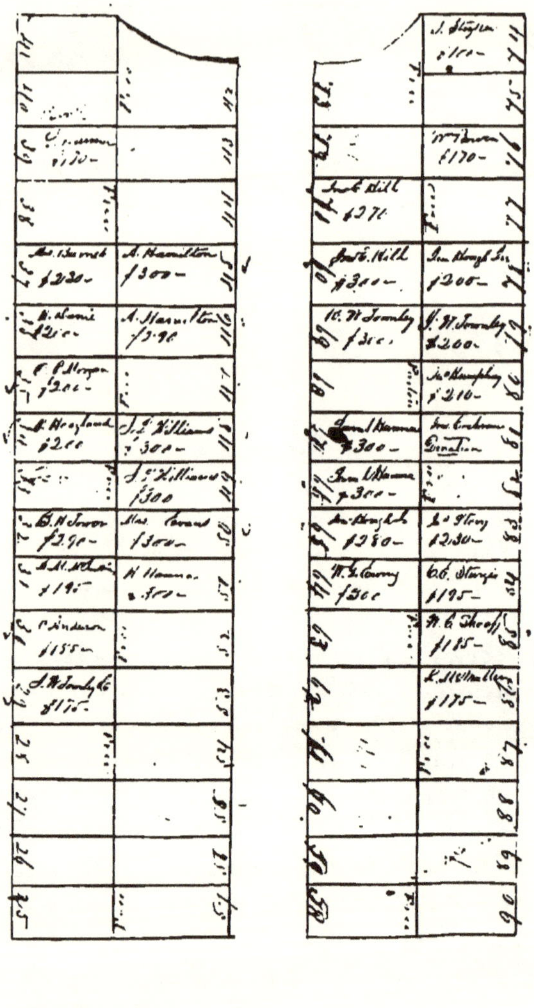

Motion J. L. Williams, Dr. W. D. W. [...]
John Hough Jr. were appointed a committee
make a report of proceedings had in the
valuation of the pews and terms of sale of
pews to be had on Thursday evening the 11th
day of November 1852.

On motion R. W. Townley, John Cochrane
and John Hough Jr were appointed a
committee to rent such pews as might
remain unsold after the public sale and
subject to rent at the rate of six per cent on their
valuation and subject to such equitable tax
as may be assessed by the Trustees from time to
time in pursuance of the resolution No 7 found
at the meeting of March 24. 1845.

Meeting then adjourned to meet in the
church Thursday evening Nov 11th 1852 at the sale
of pews.

John Hough Jr
Secretary.

At a meeting of the congregation of the 1st
Presbyterian Church of Fort Wayne held in the church
Thursday evening Nov 11th 1852 pursuant to public
notice Smallwood Noel was called to the
chair & John Hough Jr was chosen Secretary

On motion of J. L. Williams the committee
previously appointed made the following
report.

Your committee appointed at a meeting
of the Session Trustees & Building committee
held in the basement of this church on the
evening of Wednesday Nov 11th to draft a general
report of the several meetings had to ascertain
the cost of the church, fix a valuation on the
pews and arrange the terms of sale to be reported

...which the church is erected. That the committee
on valuation have taken this sum as their
basis & have fixed the valuation in accorda[nce]
with the plat reported to the meeting of Nov[?]
1852 which they present herewith for the confirmat[ion]
of this meeting Your committee also report th[e]
following terms of sale

All subscriptions actually paid either for the
erection of the building or purchase of lots t[o be]
received in payment of pews

The balance over amount subscription if
exceeding 150. to be paid ⅓ cash balance in six
months with interest but if the balance does
not exceed 150 ⅓ cash and balance in three
months with interest. Note to be given for deferred
payments without relief from valuation or
appraisement laws a discount to be made
for cash on deferred payments at the rate of
six per cent per annum.

Pews to be sold to the highest bidder but not
below the valuation of the same

No deed to be given for a pew till final payment
is made on the same.

On motion of Allen Hamilton the foregoing
report was adopted and the valuation of the
pews and terms of sale approved and fully
confirmed.

On motion of Samuel Hanna it was

Resolved that the thanks of this church
& congregation be tendered to John Cochrane
for the labor & skill bestowed by him as the
architect in the erection & completion of the
beautiful edifice now occupied by this church

On motion of John Hough Jr it was

Resolved that the resolution of the union
trustees & building committee ...

some discussion Rev Mr Edwards made
some appropriate remarks with reference to the
selling of the Pews when the Chairman
appointed Robert W Townly Salesman to sell
the pews at auction & John Hough Jr Clerk of
Sales which were to be duly marked on the
plat as registered in the minutes of the church
The sale being closed the Congregation
adjourned "sine die

John Hough Jr
Secretary.

. . . . congrega
of the First Presbyterian church of Pittsb[urgh]
On Motion Samuel Hanna was called [to]
the Chair & John Hough was chosen Secret[ary]
Rev. Mr. Lowrie then opened with Pray[er]
after which he stated the object of the
meeting to be to consider the question
of enlarging the present church edific[e]
After some discussion on the part
of Rev. Lowrie, Hanna, William
Cochrane & others On Motion of
of J. L. Williams it was

1 Resolved. 1st That, it is the sense of
this congregation that the time has
come when the enlargement of the
church edifice is expedient, and that
with gratitude to the head of the
church for that prosperity unity
and growth which makes such
enlargement, necessary we will enter
upon the work without needless delay

2 Resolved That the plan of enlargement
presented by Mr Cochrane, be adopted
subject to any minor changes
which he may find necessary or
expedient under the sanction
of the building committee

3 Resolved That the general principle
respecting, the appraisal, sale, and
renting of pews, and the levying
thereon an annual tax, the reservation
of free pews as adopted at the
Congregational meeting held March
24. 1845. be recognized as applicable
also to the addition now contemplated

4. Resolved. That for the purpose of
placing all

...essary purchase is used, at that time relinquish the same, each pewholder retaining as stock, the present assessed value of his pew or pews which together with extra sums he may have paid in the late subscription for completing the church, shall be received in payment for pews in the new building, to the extent that may be needed for his own family accommodation. All subscriptions for the enlargement shall be receivable for purchase of pews to a like extent, provided that any person or persons who object to such relinquishment have the right to retain their pew or pews, if they so elect at the sale of pews.

5. *Resolved* That in the completion of the enlargement all pews new and old about 970 in number shall be equitably appraised at their relative value as a basis for future taxation the aggregate valuation to equal their then total cost of the building, to wit the original cost thirteen thousand five hundred dollars the subsequent expenditure in completing the cupola &c Twelve Hundred dollars together with the actual cost of this addition now estimated at Sixteen thousand dollars.

6. *Resolved* That at this appraisement or the minimum, the pews be

... congregation may assess from
time to time for the Pastors sale
and other congregation expen___
and the pews remaining unsol__
to be offered at annual rent for
sum equal to such yearly tax
If at the sale or renting two or m__
persons shall select the same pe_
it shall be sold or rented to the
highest bidder.

7 <u>Resolved</u> That the building
and finance Committee proce__
immediately to circulate a subscripti
for this object, upon the basis of
these resolutions, that if possible
they contract, the whole amount
for a specific sum, and that no
contract be made until the
actual cost be first subscribed

8 <u>Resolved</u> That the following
persons constitute a building
and finance committee, to wit
John Cochrane, Samuel Hanna
Allen Hamilton, Joseph L. Actman
Henry Hoagland, Jesse L. Williams
A. B. Beaucliff C. P. Morgan and
John Hough.

After some discussion the
foregoing resolutions were put
& passed separately by a large
majority.

On motion of Samuel Hanna it
was <u>Resolved</u> That the committee
be instructed to prepare and
circulate a paper for signature
stipulating for the relinquishment

Fort Wayne Aug 3rd 1863

Pursuant to adjournment the
congregation met. Saml Hanna
in the Chair. Schultbough Secy
opened with prayer by Rev Bro
Lewie. The building & finance
committee reported that there had
been the sum of three thousand
dollars had already been subscribed
towards the extension of the church
edifice & the prospect was very
favorable for the raising of the
whole amount.

The question on the passage of
Resolutions presented at the
last meeting was then taken
up & after some discussion on
the part of Mess Humphry Ayres
Lewie Hanna. Williams and
Hough the were passed as
a whole by a large Majority
the committee then presented
the paper prepared for the
relieving instrument of pews
under Resolution No. 4
which was generally signed
Meeting then adjourned "sine die"

Schultbough
    Sec,

W. T. Williams ... the Trustees & Building
Committee Met at the office of ... &
Aug. 31. 1863 S. Hanna was chosen the
chairman & J Hough Secy
Cochrane & Humphrey & Co. the committee an offer to build the
proposed addition to the church
as follows "We propose to build a
proposed addition to the said the
church according to the plan
& specifications for the sum of six
thousand ~~dollars~~ three hundred and dollars
furnishing all the material and
labor necessary to construct said
addition" Signed Cochrane & Humphreys
which proposition was accepted
& signed by the building committee
Whereupon committee adjourned.
                        Saml Hanna
J Hough Secy   Chairman

——————————— April 20 1868.

New board of trustees. met, at the office of
John Hough present J.D. Nutman N.N. Putnam
John Hough, C.P. Morgan & L.B. Root who being
duly sworn & qualified proceed to organise
by electing J.D. Nutman President, John Hough
Secretary & N.N. Putnam Treasurer.
The salary of the Treasurer was fixed at
$200 & he was instructed to employ
Mr. Shoemaker as Sexton at a salary
of $200.

On motion of L.B. Root, C.P. Morgan and
N.N. Putnam, were appointed a committee
to contract for a superintend the change
of the North West Room of the basement
of the church into a room for the
Pastors study, and to make such
alterations & repairs in the basement
as may be required for the comfort
of the Congregation, also to select &
set out trees in the yard, to build a
cistern, to repair spouts & generally
to do such other work in & about
the building as necessity & comfort
require.

On motion adjourned on call
of the President.
John Hough
Secy.

J.D. Nutman Pt

Pursuant to Call of President, Board met at the office of John Hough, present Nutman. Hough Putnam & Root

Proceedings of last meeting read & approved. Treasurer presented the following bills Emerich $49.75 Hottewly $60.66 Myers Bros $15.31 Morgan $49.30. McDougal $118.55 Chamberlain $72.00 which were approved & ordered to be paid On Motion of Root the Treasurer was instructed to prepare a Subscription to the amount of 1500 to pay debts on which he be allowed 5 per cent for collection. On Motion of Hough, the Treasurer was instructed, to add to his Monthly Notices, a special notice to delinquents, that Pew Rents must be paid promptly, or their Pews released to other parties.
John Hough Secy.
J. D. Nutman Pt

Nov 12. 1868
Pursuant to call of President Board met, at the usual place, a full board present.
On Motion of Hough. Secretary was directed to prepare a paper to present to the congregation, stating that subscription was a failure, & an assessment was required to pay debts & to appeal to the congregation for prompt payment.

Pursuant to call of President Board
met at the office of John Hough a
Present Putman, Hough, Morgan &
Putnam.

On motion Treasurer was ordered
to notify the parties that the following
pews would be rented to other
parties, unless all arrears were
paid within thirty days from date
of notice

James Story	Pew no		125
Wm McElfatrick	"	"	124
A Wells	"	"	108
Mr Evans	"	"	62

& written notice to be served
on the parties above named
Adjourned

John Hough Secy.   S B Wilmarth

                    Decr 22. 1868

Pursuant to call Board met at the
usual place absent Root,

On Motion Secretary was ordered to
prepare a Report, for the annual
meeting, stating that through private
subscription over $2000 had been
raised & the entire indebtedness
of the church liquidated, and
recommending an assessment for
1869 of 25 per cent on Pews to pay
current expenses & to create a reserve
fund to meet extraordinary expenses

On motion Ordered to consult
the Trustees of 3d church as to
conveying to them the Lots on which
their Church is situated

in Bal of Settlmt up 1st Sept 1842   2.00

By Cash reced of E S Williams   6.00
                                     25.00
  "   "   "   " I E Kile   5.00
  "   "   "   " S Hanna   2.50
  "   "   "   " Cohran   5.00
  "   "   "   " I S W &c   3.00
                                           100.00
                                           100.00

              Bal due A J R
By Cash of Hanna   10.00
  "   "   Hamilton   10.00
  "   "   Hill   10.00   30.00
                                       70.00
By Sallery for year ending Sept 1st 1843. 500.00
                                           570.00

Dr To Recd of Borten   5.00
      Morgan & Lucy   2.00
      L S Williams   25.00
      Je Evans   5.00
      Randle   2.00
      Mores   5.00
      Richard   5.00
      Hamilton   50.00
      Page   3.00
      Sharp   2.00
      Old   3.00
      W G Ewing   10.00
      I H Jacoby   5.00
      Stewart   5.00
      Hanna   30.00
      John Cohran   10.00
      Humphrey   15.00
      of Nash & Lucas —   4.00
  "   S Hanna   5.00
      Cohran   3.00

the Other Side — Con $570.00
191.00
Bal due A.G. 373.00
To acc't of Mrs Evans 15.00
"   "   " I. Edsill — 10.00 25.00
348.00
By arties since 1843 75.00
423.00

Mr Hamilton in goods 5.00
Hanna — in acct 12.00
I Edsall — 5.00
Edwards 1.00
Cash 33.75 54.75
368.25
Rec'd M. Higins 7.00
362.25
To Note on John Kirick 40.00
327.25
Order of A Hanna 50.00
377.25

Hamilton's subscription for Allans 20.
Hanna "   "   "   " 20.
Heills "   "   "   " 10. 50.00
271.25
By cash of Sturges . 5.00
"   "   " Cochran . 7.00 12.00
259.25
r — John Edsall — 10.00
By John Leavy 8.00 249.25
" Noel 9.62
" I Coquinain 2.00
" Wm Stewart 10.00
"   " J Spencer 5.00
"   " Stokes 7.10
" Naylor 3.00
"   " B H Fawin 84.76

J. E. Zibo acct — 26
L. G. Williams — 15
A Hamilton — 15
B H Tanner — 15
J. Cochran — 16
H P Hays — 5
James Hampshire — 5 pay J Eadsale
Tuany — 5
P. Tanney acct — 16
J Hanna — 15. 37
A M Quinton — 16 — Edsal s. schall best —
acct for R M Taylor 12.12
                        137 49

The above acct with Rev A J Ranken
settled Nov 4th 1844
                        J Hanna

* 9 7 8 3 3 3 7 3 8 1 2 3 3 *